THE WOLF
WHO ONCE LOVED

ELSA MEI GESSESSE

ISBN: E-Book # 978-1-966556-77-0

      Paperback # 978-1-966556-78-7

Printed in United States of America

Disclaimer: The author and publisher make no representations or warranties with respect to the accuracy or completeness of the contents of this work and specifically disclaim all warranties, including without limitation warranties of fitness for a particular purpose. No warranty may be created or extended by sales or promotional materials. The advice and strategies contained herein may not be suitable for every situation. This work is sold with the understanding that the author and publisher are not engaged in rendering legal, accounting, or other professional services. If professional assistance is required, the services of a competent professional person should be sought.

Library of Congress Reg. # 2025910660

Cover Design by: Authors Hike

Publisher: Authors Hike

For permission requests, please contact: mcg0216@hotmail.com

Elsa ia a very talented 10 years old young lady. She lives in Las Vegas NV. She enjoys arts, music, writing, modeling and acting. She started learning Ballet at age 3. She has been learning piano and violin since age 5. She also loves drawing and painting. She has her own art studio that features all my art works. She has participated multicultural fashion shows and international beautiful you fashion tours in the past 5 years worldwide. She is the title holder of Miss Nevada. For acting, she was in a music video as well as several commercials inclu ing JW Marriott international. Additionally, she enjoys traveling around the world and getting to know diffrent cultures and traditions. She has been to 15 countries so far.

She was one of the hosts at 2024 and 2025 CCTV children's New Year gala. In addition, she did piano solo and singing at the show. She participated 2023 and 2024 Youth China international events. She was one of the lead performers as well as the host at the 2024 Youth China closing ceremony. She was one of the hosts at CCTV Media center national awards in 2023.

https://www.facebook.com/share/16erhytqqz/

Special thanks to, My school principal Dr Fisher, my 5th grade teachers Mrs Zobrist, Ms Creuziger for giving me motivation and believing in me, And my beloved family, for being there for me, wouldn't have done it without all your love and support.
Last but not least, I need to thank all my friends, especially Daphne, Gwendolyn, Mckenzie and Kleopatra who have been there for me during this journey.

I feel so greatful to have you all by my side.
Lots of love, Elsa Gessesse

Paws pounding against the earth, I can't stop. Mouth open, shoulders back, back straight. I wasn't going to break my stride. Keep running. My legs burned, my vision blurred. Don't stop.

I lifted my torn paws to the ground, forcefully pushing my body up. If I was going to run, I was going to do it right. A trot turned into a slow run. I shifted weight from my back leg to my front. The place they trapped me was not a home, it was a prison.

I looked back. The one thing I wasn't supposed to do. My nose dipped straight into the ground. Pain surged through my body, get up! I glanced behind me, nobody was chasing me.

The sun dipped below the horizon, and I lifted my nose to smell. I didn't catch any scent of a wolf, only old ones. My name was Swift for a reason.

Paws pounding against the ground, nose held high for any scent of my brother, I wasn't going to leave him to rot in that place! Mouth open, my vision was blurry, I wasn't stopping.

Let him go!' I barked, Teeth sharp, nose pointed, and growling. I couldn't get that wolf off of him. But I could try, I lunged onto the wolf, pinning him onto a rock.

He bit into my leg and I let out a yelp, I kicked him off before dashing after my brother, my stride was unsteady but I couldn't stop.

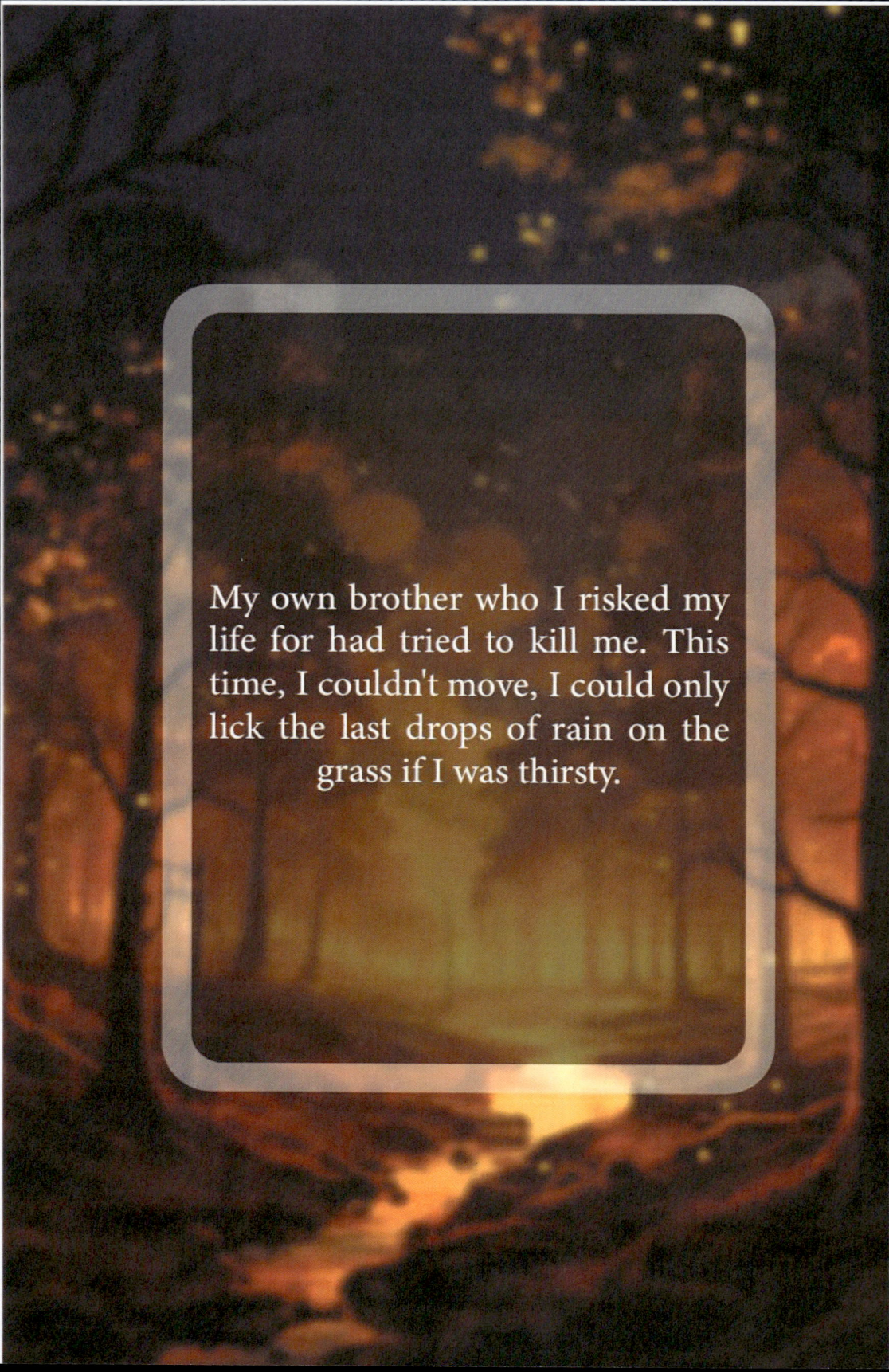

My own brother who I risked my life for had tried to kill me. This time, I couldn't move, I could only lick the last drops of rain on the grass if I was thirsty.

I laid in the grass, and closed my eyes. And let out my last howl, from deep inside my throat. Pushing back all the pain in my body for just one moment until I couldn't hold on anymore.

And finally, I could rest.